PRACTICAL JOKES

JOKES

HOW TO OUTSMART 'EM

Richard Robinson

Robinson Children's Books

First published in the UK by Robinson Children's Books,
an imprint of Constable & Robinson Ltd, 2001

Constable & Robinson Ltd
3 The Lanchesters
162 Fulham Palace Road
London W6 9ER
www.constablerobinson.com

A copy of the British Library Cataloguing in
Publication Data is available from the British Library.

ISBN 1–84119–289–9

10 9 8 7 6 5 4 3 2 1

CONTENTS

PRACTICAL JOKES 5

KEEPING VICTIMS ALIVE 6

BEST BETS 7

PERSONAL PROBLEMS 23

HALLOWEEN HAUNTS 39

NASTY PASTI 55

SOUNDS 'ORRID 65

FIENDISH FOOD 87

TAKING IT FOR GRANTED 105

SECRECY 115

I SPEAK YOUR FATE 125

CARD AND BOUNDER 139

IT MUST BE MAGIC 147

SHOW TIME 157

THE CHAPTER OF HORRORS 175

GOTCHA!!! 189

PRACTICAL JOKES

Here's heaps of gags and tricks to play on your friends and family. See the symbols at the bottom of each page.

Some are dead easy

Some are a little harder

Some need preparation

Some can be done straight away

Some need grown-ups to help

KEEPING VICTIMS ALIVE

It really makes no sense to bump them off, does it! Eventually you're going to run out of people to do tricks on. That's plain clumsy. To keep a steady supply of victims, make sure they stay alive, enjoy the tricks and come back for more.

Watch them carefully while you do the tricks. If they start to show signs of distress – sweating, shaking, steam coming out of their ears – then back away. Treat them with respect. Offer them a biscuit.

And when they find the biscuit's made of painted plaster, don't laugh too loud.

Don't forget – check with a grown-up before you start; they can be helpful in finding the things you need and prevent any accidents.

BEST BETS

MAKE NO PROFIT

To trick somebody is one thing, to walk away
with the contents of their pocket is quite
another. They might forgive you for the trick,
but not for taking money off them. Don't use
your tricks to make money. These Betchas
work best when given free.

BETCHA YOU CAN'T ANSWER FOUR QUESTIONS WRONG

Say you're going to ask four questions, and they must answer all of them wrong. Ask:

"WHAT'S YOUR NAME?"

"HOW OLD ARE YOU?"

"WHAT COLOUR IS YOUR HAIR?"

...Then look puzzled;

"...UM, IS THAT THREE QUESTIONS I'VE ASKED?"

"YES," they answer.

"... AND THAT WAS THE FOURTH - GOTCHA!"

BETCHA I CAN MAKE THE QUEEN SMILE

I never think the queen looks too happy on those bank notes. If I owned a country I'd have a pretty big grin on my face. Let's make her happier.

Fold a bank note like this.

When you look at her from below she'll have a proper smirk.

Look at her from above – now she looks even more miserable than before.

BETCHA I CAN DOUBLE YOUR MONEY

Simple – just put a fiver in your pocket. When you put it in you double it, and when you bring it out you find it increases (In creases, geddit?).

OK. Bad joke. Do this instead;

Cut your note along the middle, then fold as shown.

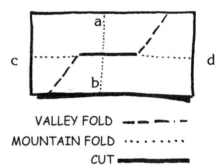

When you fold it cleverly, it looks like two.

VALLEY FOLD   — — — · —

MOUNTAIN FOLD   · · · · · · · ·

CUT   ━━━━

BETCHA I CAN FIND SOMETHING IN THIS ROOM WHICH YOUR LEFT HAND CAN HOLD BUT YOUR RIGHT HAND CAN'T

The important part of this gag is the phrase "in this room". Your victim will look all round the room before accepting the bet.

Take their left hand and place it on their right elbow.

GOTCHA!

BETCHA I CAN TAKE A BISCUIT FROM UNDER A CUP WITHOUT TOUCHING THE CUP

This is a great gag, because your victim actually helps you.

Put the cup over the biscuit.

Do some magical noises and arm wavings.

Say, "there you are... ... ... Do you want to check?"

Your victim won't believe you and will pick up the cup...

That's when you take the biscuit.

GOTCHA!

BETCHA I CAN PUSH SOMEBODY THROUGH THE HANDLE OF A MUG

Select the smallest person in the room (probably a girl), to make it easy. Make her stand sideways on, so that you can push her through the handle easier.

Ask her to take a deep breath, pull her tummy right in, count to three then...

Stick your finger through the handle and push her.

BETCHA I CAN MAKE YOU SAY "BLACK" WITHIN A MINUTE

Set a stopwatch ticking, then the conversation runs like this:

"WHAT'S THE OPPOSITE OF DARK?"

"LIGHT."

"WHAT'S THE OPPOSITE OF UP?"

"DOWN."

"WHAT'S THE OPPOSITE OF FRONT?"

"BACK."

"THERE, THAT DIDN'T TAKE LONG."

"WHAT DO YOU MEAN?"

"YOU SAID IT!"

"NO I DIDN'T, I SAID 'BACK'."

"EXACTLY. I WIN."

"NO. YOU SAID YOU WERE GOING TO MAKE ME SAY 'BLACK'."

"WELL... (looking at stopwatch) ...YOU SAID IT NOW!"

BETCHA I CAN PREDICT HEADS OR TAILS EVERY TIME

When you toss a coin, it's equally likely to come down heads as tails. So if you guess it, you're going to be correct half the time, right?

Wrong! This is what you do. Use a 2p coin.

1. Flip it, catch it, then slap it on the other hand, ready to show it.

2. But before you slap it down, stroke the coin with your thumb.

3. On a 2p coin the tails side is rougher.

4. You can tell which way up the coin is from that.

NEEDS:- 2p COIN

BETCHA I CAN ... MAKE YOU TURN YOUR HANDS OVER

Another classic.

"BET YOU I CAN MAKE YOU TURN YOUR HANDS OVER."

  "BET YOU CAN'T."

"LET'S SEE. FIRST OF ALL, HOLD OUT YOUR HANDS."

(victim does so)

"NO THE OTHER WAY UP."

(victim turns hands over)

"GOTCHA!"

BETCHA I KNOW WHAT YOU ARE GOING TO SAY NEXT

There is only one way to do this, and even then it's risky. But when it works it's brilliant. Pick your victim carefully and say exactly this:

"I know what you are going to say next."

Victim says, "What?"

You pull a piece of paper from your pocket. On it is written...

BETCHA I CAN...STAND ON MY HANDS FOR A MINUTE

To win the bet, do this.

You look stupid, but they *feel* stupid.

THE FAMOUS TROUSERS-DOWN WAGER

One morning Mick went up to his foreman. "Are you a betting man?" he asked.

The foreman said, "depends on the bet".

"Well," said Mick, "I'll bet you ten pounds you can't remember what colour underpants you put on this morning."

"That's easy," said the foreman. They shook on it. "I put on red underpants this morning."

"Prove it," said Mick.

The foreman pulled down his trousers to reveal his red pants. Mick was strangely happy to hand over a tenner. As he did so a groan went up from the other men on site. You see, Mick had bet them *each* a tenner that he could get the foreman to pull down his trousers before lunch.

BETCHA CAN'T EAT THREE CRACKERS IN A MINUTE

No trickery here.

It really is impossible. Normally your saliva helps to turn food slimy enough to slip down your throat. But crackers are so-o-o-o dry. The first cracker takes up all the saliva. The second makes your mouth drier than the Sahara. Chomping on the third is like demolishing a house in a sand storm. The victim will be still trying to clear his mouth five minutes later.

NEEDS:- 3 CRACKERS

DID YOU LOSE? PAY THEM TOMORROW

Never bet for real money. If you do bet and lose, tell them you'll pay them back tomorrow.

The next day;

"CAN I HAVE MY MONEY?"

"- WHAT DAY IS IT TODAY?"

"THURSDAY."

"- THAT'S TODAY IS IT?"

"YES."

"- SO IT'S NOT TOMORROW?"

"NO."

"WELL, COME BACK TOMORROW AND I'LL PAY YOU."

PERSONAL
PROBLEMS

Some tricks you can play with your own body.

LEFT LEG LEGS IT

Make your left leg disappear, just like that!

Hold your coat or a towel in front of your legs, like this:

Put on your best showman act. To carry this off you need a lot of pizzaz. Lift the coat twice to reveal your legs. The third time one of them has gone!

Believe me, it works.

NEEDS:- TOWEL OR COAT

STICK A PEN UP YOUR NOSE

Firstly, let's make one thing clear; NEVER STICK A PEN UP YOUR NOSE!

Now let's pretend to do it. Use a plain-sided pen or pencil.

Place the very tip of the blunt end in your nose.

When you push the hand up, the pen slips down into your palm, but it seems to go right up into your brain.

NEEDS:- BLUNT PENCIL

HEAD BANGER

Bash your head against the door, no problem.

Do this whenever you're frustrated. Your head never quite touches the door, but your foot kicks it, and it sounds like your head. OUCH!

NEEDS:- DOOR

COCKING A SLOW SNOOK

Hold your hands
and arms out to
the side, as in
the drawing.

Now ask your
victim to slowly
push down each
elbow.

When the elbows
are pushed right
down, stick out
your tongue,
blow a raspberry
and wiggle your
fingers.

DOORWAY DRAMA

Get a grip!

Gotta go now! A hand
appears from nowhere
and drags you off.

Stand in the doorway
with your shoulder just
– only just – out of
view. Your hand
appears and grabs
your hair, then pulls it,
and you, out of view.

SELF-LOVE: THE CARESS

From the back it looks as if someone's snogging you.

From the front we can see you're just sad!

STRETCHING CREDIBILITY

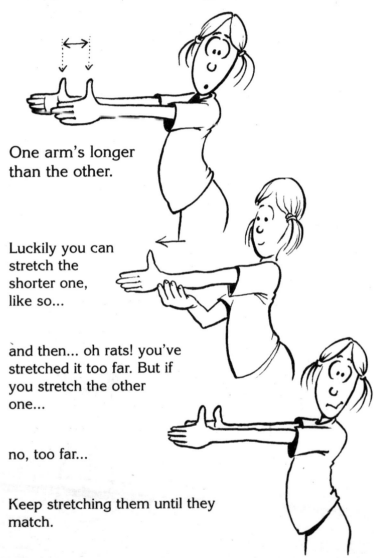

One arm's longer
than the other.

Luckily you can
stretch the
shorter one,
like so...

and then... oh rats! you've
stretched it too far. But if
you stretch the other
one...

no, too far...

Keep stretching them until they
match.

BROKEN ARM

Hold your arm out sideways and let your forearm relax completely. It will swing like a pendulum. Give the forearm a little push, so it swings right round, then subsides again. With practice it will look completely dead.

WARTY HANDSHAKE

When you shake somebody's hand, bend your middle finger in.

Say, "excuse my wart" while you do it.

BROKEN NOSE

Hold your nose like this:

When you bend it from side to side, they can hear it click. That's broken all right!

You've got your thumbnail in your mouth, flicking your front teeth to make the click sound.

HACKED FINGER

Cut out the bottom of a matchbox to make it look like this. Now turn it the right way up.

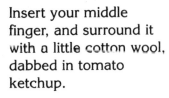

Insert your middle finger, and surround it with a little cotton wool, dabbed in tomato ketchup.

Close the box.

Put a pained expression on your face and run to Mum. "Have you got any glue? I've had an accident with the kitchen knife."

Open the matchbox.

Is there room for one more in the ambulance?

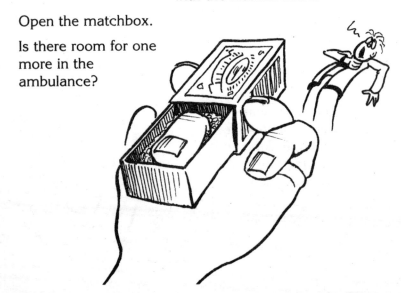

NEEDS:- MATCHBOX, SCISSORS, COTTON WOOL, TOMATO SAUCE

NICKED FINGER

You can remove bits of yourself, no problem.

This is how you hold your hands.

The tip of one finger attaches to the bottom of the other.

The finger hides the join.

Slide the tip off a little way, then slide it back.

Be quick! If they look too hard, they'll spot the trick.

NOSE NICKING

Don't try this on grown-ups. With two-year-olds it might just work.

Pretend to steal their nose.

Show them you've got it, like this.

If they reach up to check, consider yourself a success. You pulled it off!

HIGH TREASON

Pranksters sometimes use newspapers to do their tricks.

John Holt was only 145 cm tall, and felt embarrassed socially. Imagine how excited he was when he saw an advertisement in the paper, "You can be four centimetres taller! – send £9.90 for our book *Height is Might*, showing you a revolutionary way to increase your height." He quickly sent off his £9.90 and awaited the dawn of a new life. Eventually the book arrived. It was a thick book. In between two of the pages was a slip of paper which read simply, "Stand on this book."

This advertisement in another paper appealed to people's greed: "Get rich quick!", it said. "Send £15.00 and I will tell you in one simple lesson how to make a fortune." Many people sent in the £15.00, keen to make a quick million. They received a letter with the advice; "Do as I did."

MAD BAD GAGS FROM RAG WEEK

Students have a special week in which they play tricks on each other. One Rag Week, a student warned some road workers that some of his friends were dressing up as policemen. "They're going to try to stop you digging up the road."

"Well we won't let them," said the labourers.

The student phoned the police; "Look, there are some students out here digging up the road. They're dressed like labourers, but I think they should be stopped, don't you?"

The student and his friends sat up in a college window and watched the chaos that followed.

HALLOWEEN HAUNTS

Trick Or Treat tricks.

Halloween is the day when all the ancient spirits roam free around the town. Well, if you sit there and wait for them to come and haunt you, you'll be in for a pretty dreary evening, so get out there and do your own haunting.

D-D-DO YOU BELIEVE IN HUMANS?

KNOCKER SHOCKER

Tie one end of a piece of thread to your victim's door knocker. Hide, holding the other end.

Pull on the thread so the knocker knocks.

Hide so that when the door is answered – there's no one there!

As soon as the door is closed, knock again.

It's amazing! Once again there's nobody there. Each time the door is shut, knock on it again.

NEEDS:- STRING

CREEPY CRAWLIES

Tell your victim it's time for a small haunting.

Run the forefingers of both hands down her face gently. Do it about three times. Mind her eyes.

It's important to close the eyes to protect them.

Run your fingers down her face again – but this time use two fingers from THE SAME hand.

The other hand is now free to tickle the back of your victim's head.

Quickly bring the hands back together, so that when she opens her eyes the two hands are in front.

So whooooooo did the tickling?

TORCHLIGHT TERRORS

How to light up your face.

How do you light up your face from below? It seems so simple, but it's easy to get it wrong.

Remember, your eyes must be lit up – so if you aren't dazzling yourself, adjust the torch until you do.

Practise in front of a mirror to get it absolutely spot-on

TORCHLIGHT TERRORS II
THE GIANT HAND

Throw a shadow of your hand on the ceiling.

Move your hand towards the torch. The shadow hand gets bigger and bigger and... grabs you all. Don't forget the spooky sounds.

THINGS THAT GO BUMP

P-p-petrify the p-p-parents.

Fill a cup or bowl with dried peas. Right to the top. Almost spilling out. Put it on an up-turned baking tray, in a cupboard in your parents' bedroom.

Just before they go to bed, half fill the cup with water. All night long your parents will be spooked by sounds of tapping.

As the peas at the bottom absorb the water they swell, pushing the peas at the top out of the cup. Which drop onto the baking tray ... spik ... spok ... spik ... spok ...

MAKING UP

Make your face even more ugly than usual.

Paint drips of blood leaking from the bottom of your eyes.

Paint eyes on your closed eyelids.

Paint a single bullet hole on your forehead, with a trickle of blood.

Paint a false mouth and crazy teeth right across your face.

Use black make-up to paint a skull on your face.

Use two half-pingpong balls to give yourself boggly eyes.

NEEDS:- FACE PAINTS, PINGPONG BALL

BLACK TEETH

Take care what you put in your mouth.
Don't blacken your teeth with paint.
Use black cardboard.

Once it's damp it will snuggle up to
the tooth and won't slip out. And
don't forget to smile.

THE ALIEN – YOUR STOMACH ERUPTS

There are fancy ways to do this, but here's the simplest. You must wear your floppiest top – big woolly pulley, fleece, cardigan, whatever.

Pull your arm out of one of the sleeves and rest your hand on your tummy.

Hold the empty sleeve so it doesn't look empty.

Now stare aghast at your front. Move your spare hand about. Something's trying to break out of your stomach!

Punch your hand out, and scream!

"It's hatching!"

HEAR 'EM SCARE 'EM – GIVE 'EM SCORPION EGGS

You learn a lot about human nature here. People love to live dangerously. Give them an envelope which says "Don't look in here!" and it will be open in seconds. Even if it's got scorpion eggs in.

Find a tame grown-up. You need a piece of wire coathanger, cut and bent exactly like this:

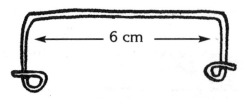

You also need two elastic bands and a washer (that's a metal washer, not a clothes washer).

Fit the elastic bands on the wire and the washer like this.

Prepare an envelope; write warnings all over it – "BEWARE – SCORPION EGGS". Do the same to a piece of paper.

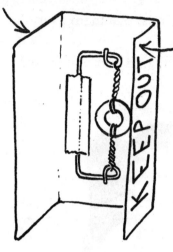

Fold the paper in three, so it fits neatly into the envelope.

Stick the wire gizmo onto the centre panel.

Wind up the washer and hold in place while you

fold the paper over. Keep holding it while you slip the paper into the envelope.

The envelope holds the washer in place. But as soon as some curious soul takes a peek inside the envelope, the washer rattles noisily...

The scorpions have hatched!

NEEDS:- WIRE COATHANGER, WIRE CUTTERS, 2 ELASTIC BANDS, METAL WASHER, ENVELOPE, PAPER

THE ELASTIC BAND HORROR FACE

If you have a few big elastic bands, pull them over your face.

Don't smile. They might ping off and hurt your nose.

THE HEADLESS TORSO

A simple effect, but best seen in bad light –
outside at night.

Pull your pullover over your head.
Stumble about, moaning "I've got a
terrible headache."

Deluxe version – get a friend to tuck
their head under your arm. Now they
can do the moaning.

NEEDS:- LARGE PULLOVER

HALLOWEEN GOODBYE WEEN! – THE KIDNAP!

This one works best in the dark.

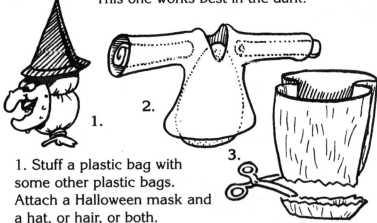

1. Stuff a plastic bag with some other plastic bags. Attach a Halloween mask and a hat, or hair, or both.

2. Find an old pullover. Stuff the sleeves with rolled-up newspaper and the body with a pillow or cushion.

3. Cut the bottom off a sack or big bin liner.

Now get your friend to help put that lot together.

4. Attach the bottom of the pullover to your waist with a belt or string.

5. Pull the arms behind your back and tie the sleeve ends together.

NEEDS:- PLASTIC BAGS, HALLOWEEN MASK, HAT OR HAIR, OLD PULLOVER

5.

6. Pull the sack over your head. The bottom sits around your waist, under the sleeves, the top should sit around your neck, so that only your head is showing. (Tie the top round with sticky tape.)

6.

7.

7. One of your hands in the sack grips the collar of the pullover and the neck of the head.

It looks as if a Halloween witch is stealing you away in a sack on her back. Don't forget to cry for help.

Bet you I can push myself under that door.

Surely only a fool would fall for this one
... Now you will find how many fools
there are in the world.

See p192 for the answer.

NASTI PASTI

Playing with your food
Before it plays with you.

DO AS I DRINK

To beat you at this game, your opponent must do exactly the same as you. Sit facing each other with a glass of drink in front of you both, as if you are looking in a mirror.

Now do some moves. Your opponent must do the same.

Pick up the glass – Lift it right over your head.

Bring it down again – Say "Cheers!"

Take a swig – Swallow it. Pass it to the other hand.

Lift it right up again – Lower it again.

Say "Cheers!" again. So far so easy!

Take a swig – don't swallow it.

Pass it to the other hand.

Bring it up to your mouth.

Spit the mouthful out again.

Your opponent won't be able to do that!

SLIME-BALL

Cornflour has a strange way with it. When it is knocked about it stays solid, but when it stops moving it turns liquid.

Try it: Mix some cornflour with a little water, stirring slowly all the time. When it looks nice and liquid, pick up a lump of it and toss it between your hands. Keep it moving as you approach your victim and hand it over.

As soon as it's in a hand that's not moving, it'll dribble to the floor.

Careful where you do this. Don't do it over the TV – you'll ruin it. Do it over something you don't need.

NEEDS:- BOWL, CORNFLOUR, WATER

HOW TO EAT A GOLDFISH

Get a grown-up to cut a thin slice out of a carrot.

Cut it down to goldfish shape. Use a felt-tip pen to put a dot on either side for eyes.

Hide it in your hand when you go to your friend's house. Show an interest in their goldfish. Say: "They're such lovely colours aren't they. I wonder if they taste as good as they look. Shall I find out?"

Dip the hand with the carrot in the water and come out wiggling the thing, before slipping it into your mouth.

Your friend will make a face like a goldfish.

Show them how you did the trick QUICKLY, before they go find the harpoon.

NEEDS:- CARROT, KNIFE, FELT-TIP PEN

FLOATING BUN

It needn't be a bun, it could be a banana, an apple, a potato, a shrunken head, anything you can stick on a fork.

Well, go ahead, stick it on a fork.

Hold a hanky, scarf or tea towel in front of you. The complicated bit is, you have to hold the thing-on-a-fork as well. Do it like the drawing.

Nobody can see you're holding the fork.

It is important that you practise in front of the mirror until the fork disappears.

When you twitch the fork, the bun-apple-potato-banana makes a mysteeeeeerious bump in the scarf. When you twitch the fork another way, the thingy rises into view, then sinks again – Spooky!

No, really, it works!

NEEDS:- BUN, SCARF OR TEA TOWEL, FORK

NOSEY PARKING

The Sticky Teaspoon.

For goodness sake, get a life! Or else stick a teaspoon on your nose.

Get a teaspoon, breathe on it for a second, then place it on your nose. If you get it right it'll stay there.

Promise.

SPOON BENDING

Can you bend a spoon and return it to its
original shape intact?

Hold a dessertspoon
like this – note the
overlapping fingers in
the middle.

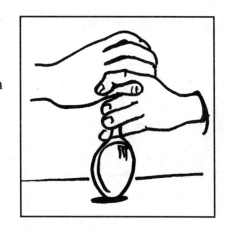

Push it down against
the table to bend it,
then bend it back.

But this is what you
actually do...

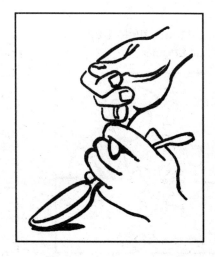

THIS APPLE'S GONE SOFT

Follow the pictures and it'll seem as if the apple has bounced on the floor like a ball.

1. Examine the apple.

2. Throw it down to the floor – but don't let go!

 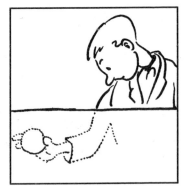

3. Instead, flick it up with your fingers.

4. Catch it with your other hand.

NEEDS:- APPLE, SHEET OR TABLE TO HIDE YOUR ARMS

BUN WITH DOUGH IN IT

Hide a £2 coin in your hand.

Hold a bun in both hands, pressing the coin against it.

Break it half open by pressing down.

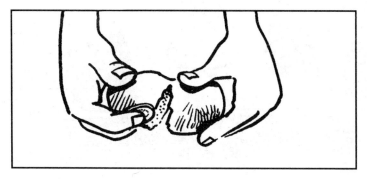

Press the coin into the gap.

Now finish breaking it open by pressing up.

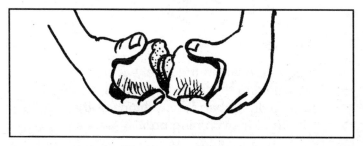

The coin will seem to pop out of it. Do it again. And again – all the buns have coins in them!

Sell your magic buns for £1 each.

NEEDS:- £2 COIN, BUN

Bet you I can sing under water.

Your victim will immediately accept the bet, thinking that even if you win, you'll have to do embarrassing things at the bottom of a swimming pool.

How do you do it?

See p190 for the answer.

SOUNDS
'ORRID

All sounds that happen in the wrong place are 'orrid. The soft tones of monks' chanting won't win any fans on Top of the Pops, and Hip Hop Rap won't go down well in a monastery at two in the morning.

Even the soft sound of ripping cloth can cause terror in the right place at the right time, as you will find.

BREAKING THE SOUND BARRIER

Make your own supersonic plane.

Fold a piece of paper like this:

Fold in half to find the centre line.

Unfold.

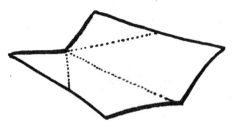

Fold the top edge in to the centre line.

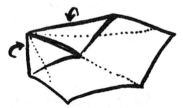

Fold the new edges in likewise.

Fold about 3 cm of the
bottom side up.

Fold over your Concorde
and draw in the cockpit.

To break the sound barrier, hold it by the nose and
swing it downwards as fast as possible.

FART MACHINE

Make a square of paper from an ordinary piece like this:

Fold one edge over against its neighbour.

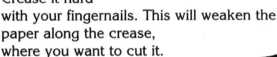

Fold up the remaining tab. Crease it hard with your fingernails. This will weaken the paper along the crease, where you want to cut it.

Extra tip – lick along the very edge of the crease; this weakens it even more. Now, when you pull it apart, the tab will come clean away, leaving the square.

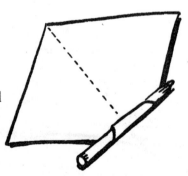

Roll up the paper round a pen – DIAGONALLY. Let the pen drop out and secure the tube with a dab of sticky tape.

Use a pair of scissors
to cut around the top,
almost but not quite
completely.

Bend up the tab that
you've just made.

When you suck gently
on the other end, you
get a soft, succulent
thrrrrrrp.

If you don't get a rich
and fruity noise first
time, keep trying a
little softer, or a little
harder.

NEEDS:- PIECE OF PAPER, PEN, SCISSORS, STICKY TAPE

MORE GOOD VIBRATIONS

Press your mouth against your arm and blow. Where it escapes, it will make the flesh vibrate – more fruity noises.

Try this...

or this...

or this...

PUMP SQUEAK

Bike pumps can build up higher pressure than your lungs, so the note will be higher. With a bike pump you can do ear-piercing squeals and squeaks.

BALLOON SQUEAK

Blow up a balloon.

Pull the neck tight. As the air squeezes out it squeals like a pig.

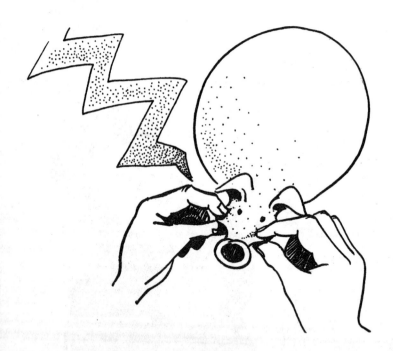

THE WHOOPEE CUSHION

Remove the top from an old washing-up liquid bottle.

Cut the end off a balloon. Attach it to the neck of the bottle.

Attach a peg. Practise squeezing the bottle to find the best peg position for a good thrrrrrp.

Put it under a cushion. Wait patiently.

NEEDS:- WASHING-UP LIQUID BOTTLE, BALLOON, SCISSORS, PEG

CUSTOMIZE YOUR BIKE

Use a clothes peg to attach a playing card to the fork of your bike. As the wheel turns the card will catch in the spokes to make a roar like a motor bike.

Card warning: Don't take cards from a full pack. Ask a parent – every home has a pack of cards with one missing, which means the other fifty-one are useless anyway.

NEEDS:- CLOTHES PEG, PLAYING CARD

COMB KAZOO

The cheapest instrument in the world. Fold a piece of grease-proof or tracing paper over a comb. When you sing a note with your mouth touching the paper two things happen; a) you get a brassy sound, b) it's unbearably ticklish.

SPOOKY OWL CALL

This is a hard one to get, but I have known real owls fooled by the sound.

Cup your hands.

Blow between your thumbs, downwards, as shown.

Adjust the angle and the pressure between the thumbs until a hooting sound comes. Keep at it. You'll get there in the end – what else is there to do anyway?

GRASS WHISTLE

Put a piece of grass between your thumbs and blow. The grass vibrates and rasps.

The same idea lies behind the clarinet, oboe and bassoon – all called "reed" instruments because they have a piece of reed in the mouthpiece, which squawks in the same way, though a little bit classier. Actually, your voice is made the same way – a piece of vibrating cartilage in your throat makes the squeaks that your mouth turns into words.

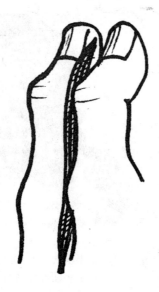

NEEDS:- GRASS

SOCCER WHISTLE – THE ULTIMATE DETERRENT

This is the big one. Master this and you can be heard half way round the world.
The fingers push the tongue back on itself. Keep adjusting position and pressure til the sound comes.

BROKEN NECK

This will get you off games, work, conscription into the army, jury service, washing-up duty, homework, anything.

Put a plastic cup in your armpit.

Say, "I'm sorry, I can't help with games/ work/ the army/ jury service/ washing-up duty/ homework. I hurt my neck yesterday."

Pull your head sideways and at the same time squeeze the glass with your arm. It will sound like your head is about to drop off. You'll be in hospital in no time.

NEEDS:- PLASTIC CUP

NAUGHTY BUT KNIFE

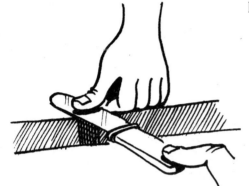

Press a knife blade on the table, flick the handle. It twangs! Slide it about to make the twang change pitch.

Boiiiing

FORK VENTRILOQUISM

Throw a ping across the table.

Hold the fork just above the table.

Pinch the prongs to make a "ping" sound. When you lower the bottom of the fork to touch the table the sound gets louder. (The vibrating fork gets the table to join in.)

Pretend to throw the ping at your victim as the fork touches the table. PING coming over!

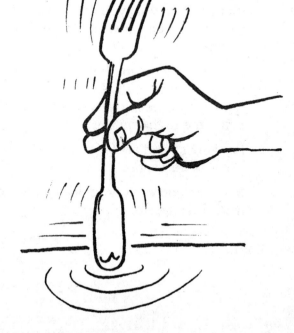

SPOON TOONS

This isn't noise, it's music!

Hold two metal spoons like this. Hold them as firmly as you can. There should be a small gap between the bowls of the spoons.

However tightly you hold them, if you tap them against your knee they'll clack together. So keep clacking and you can beat time to the music.

Hold your hand above them and you can clack twice as fast.

Run them down your knuckles and you have a glissando.

The professionals do this:

Clack against the heel of the hand...

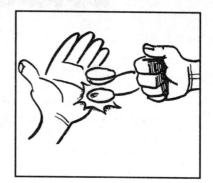

... and the knee with one stroke.

As the spoons rise, turn the hand and clack against the base of the thumb.

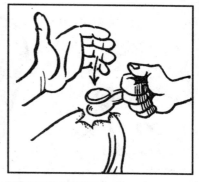

Turn the hand as the spoons drop – clack against the heel of the hand and the knee again.

And so on. With a little practice you can get a really fast spoon roll going.

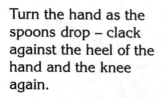

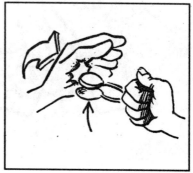

NEEDS:- 2 METAL SPOONS

RIPPING FUN

Anyone in your home like gardening?
Stick a piece of cloth in your pocket
and follow them around the garden until
they bend down, then rip the cloth
behind their back. Watch them blush.

NEEDS:- PIECE OF OLD CLOTH

POP CORN

You need indigestion tablets. If you have been doing your practical jokes properly, everyone in your house has indigestion. Borrow one of their tablets.

Find an old film container and stick the tablet inside the lid with some Blutac. Put a teaspoon of water in the pot. Put the lid on. While it stays the right way up nothing happens. If it is turned over so that the water gets to the tablet, there is a short silence, then the pot explodes and goes flying in the air. It's quite harmless, makes no mess, and gives a small and perfectly formed shock.

Bet you can't push me off a sheet of paper.

Is it possible that a big feller and a little feller can both stand on a sheet of newspaper, and the big feller can't push the little feller off?

FIENDISH FOOD

The best bad cooking.

For those of you who think your parents' cooking is a joke anyway, this chapter holds no surprises.

BAKED BEAN CAKE

I will leave you to make the cake from a standard recipe, or buy one ready made.

To make the beans, roll some marzipan into little balls. The chips are also made from marzipan. To make them look more realistic you can paint the beans and chips with a little food colouring – brown will make the chips look cooked.*

*(Brown is made by mixing yellow and red and, if possible, black.)

The baked bean sauce effect is made like this: Make some water ice, by mixing 50 gms sifted icing sugar with the juice of half a lemon. Add a little water, then a little more, until it pours like thick gravy. Add some orange (yellow and red) food colouring to make it baked bean colour.

Pour it over the beans and the cake will look as if it's covered with real baked beans and chips.

NEEDS:- SPONGE CAKE, MARZIPAN, FOOD COLOURING, WATER, LEMON JUICE, ICING SUGAR

WORM SANDWICH

An ideal birthday cake for Mum; a sandwich full of squirmy wormies. She'll love it!

If you want to be really flash, make the "bread" out of two layers of cake, cut to look like bread.

Otherwise, just use a couple of slices of real bread, spread with butter and honey or jam (to stick the worms down).

To make the worms you need a fistful of marzipan. Add some black and a little red to make the worm a greyish pink colour.

(I know you think worms are bright pink, but look at one and you'll see it's basically very dull.)

Mush the marzipan up so the colour spreads evenly, then make worms.

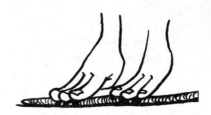

Here's the clever bit: roll them down a comb.

Those ridges will make them look totally real.

Arrange them squirmily in the bread.

If Mum likes it she might share her worms with you.

NEEDS:- 2 SLICES OF BREAD OR CAKE, BUTTER, JAM OR HONEY, MARZIPAN, FOOD COLOURING, COMB

MAGGOTTY APPLES

Now you know how to make
worms, (see Worm Sandwich,
p90), you can infect the fruit
bowl. Put the worms all over
the fruit. Bore small holes
in a couple of the
apples and insert
the worms in
those.

NEEDS:- MARZIPAN, FOOD COLOURING

WORM SOUP

Cook some spaghetti.

Put some warm water in a
bowl, mix in a teaspoon of
bicarbonate of soda (used
for cooking). Now add the
spaghetti and watch. It
starts to move! As
bubbles form, they
push and pull
the spaghetti
strands about,
and make it
look
alive.

NEEDS:- SPAGHETTI, WARM WATER, BICARBONATE OF SODA

FANGS FOR THE MEMORIES

Take a piece of orange peel, push it inside out. Insert in mouth. Done!

Extra deluxe version; cut some teeth out with a knife.

SELF-SLICING BANANA

Borrow a needle.

Push it into the banana as far as the opposite skin. Wiggle it from side to side. It cuts through the banana, but leaves only a tiny pin hole behind.

Do the same up and down the banana. Now, when you peel your magic banana, it is ready-sliced for your guests.

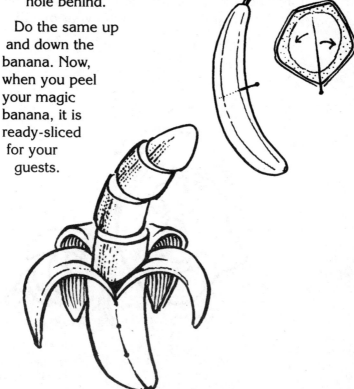

PHANTOM BANANA

Finish
the banana, then
push the banana skin
towards your mouth. At the
same time, push your tongue into
your cheek. If you time it right (practise
in front of the mirror) it'll look as if the ghost
banana has gone right through your mouth.

I SCREAM

Make a tub of mashed potato. Leave it in the fridge
for a while, then spoon dollops out into bowls
and deliver them to your guests, with
chocolate sauce, sprinkles and a
wafer in each. They won't
accept any more
invitations from
Y O U !

NEEDS:- MASHED POTATO, SUNDAE DISHES, DECORATIONS

MARZIPAN SPUDS

Make a
spud out of
marzipan.
Put it in the
middle of a
bowl of
proper
boiled
potatoes.
Wait now,
be patient.
It won't
be long.

NEEDS:- MARZIPAN, DISH OF BOILED POTATOES

BANANAS IN BANANAS

Buy a big banana and a small one. Open the big one carefully at the wrong end and remove the pith. (Leave as much of the skin as possible intact.) Slip the whole small banana inside. When you peel the banana you find a banana!

NEEDS:- LARGE BANANA, SMALL BANANA

LITTLE AND LARGE

Next time you go to the supermarket,
find two bananas the same size. Hold one
above the other and ask the assistant
which is larger. He'll point to the lower
one, because It really does look
larger – it's an optical illusion.

"Are you sure it's the largest?"
you ask. "Yes," he says.

Now hold the "bigger"
one above the other
one. Suddenly it isn't
bigger any more.

"Are you SURE?"

"Yes," he says.
"No!" he says.
"What's gone
wrong with
my brain!"
he says.

NEEDS:- 2 BANANAS THE SAME SIZE

L-EYE-CHEES

Lychees will never taste the same after this.

Take as many as you like, dry the outsides on some tissue, paint an iris on each with some blue food colour, using the hole as the pupil. Paint the backs red to look like blood vessels.

Leave them around the plate. They look like eyes.

...If they follow you around the room, run for it.

NEEDS:- TINNED LYCHEES, TISSUE, FOOD COLOURING

ENOUGH VEGETABLES TO SEE YOU THROUGH THE WEEK

If
you look really
hard – squint a little –
many vegetables seem to
have a face. Make the most of
it; scoop a little dip where the
eyes might be and put a lychee
in each one.

Go further, why not; place a
glacé cherry where its
nose should be.

GREEN EGGS AND HAM – COLOURED FOOD

The
best way
to keep all the
food for yourself at a
party. Soak some hard-boiled
eggs in green food colouring. Mix blue
food colouring with the mashed potato, put
green colouring with the lemonade. Put
black food colouring in the jelly.
Serve this lot up to your
guests and watch the
colour drain from
their faces.

NEEDS:- HARD-BOILED EGGS, FOOD COLOURING, MASHED POTATO, LEMONADE

DINING GLOOM

In the depths of the ocean, where it
is pitch black, fishes will often see a
tasty looking worm glowing in the
darkness. As they swim towards the
snack they discover too late that it
isn't a worm at all, but a cunningly
shaped fin on the front of the
"angler" fish. In a microsecond they
find THEY are the snack.

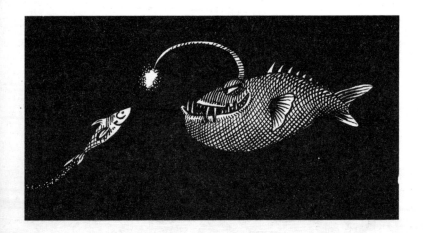

TAKING IT FOR GRANTED

Most tricks involve catching people off-guard. Which isn't difficult. Life is too short to check everything. A biscuit is a biscuit is a biscuit, right? Wrong! Read on ...

FALSE FOOD

Buy a sweet. Remove the wrapping carefully, eat the contents, then refold the wrapping to look like the original.

Don't offer it, just leave it out somewhere on its own.

Before long someone will spot it and try to eat it.

TEA-HEE

Offer to make your Mum or Dad a cup of tea.

But actually make them a cup of coffee.

So long as they're expecting tea, they'll get a shock from their first mouthful.

Strangely, once they get used to the fact that it's coffee they'll probably be quite happy to carry on. You won't have to leave the country in a hurry.

INSIDE STORY

Try some swaps.

Open some crisp packets carefully from below. Take the crisps out and put some Cornflakes in before resealing

Or leave the crisps in, but add a couple of lettuce leaves and a note:

DON'T FORGET TO EAT YOUR GREENS - MUM

Or open several different packs and swap the pickle flavour crisps with the smokey cheese, etc. See if anyone spots the difference. I bet they don't.

NEEDS:- PACKET OF CRISPS, CORNFLAKES, LETTUCE, PEN, PAPER, GLUE

CHOC-CHIP SPOOKIES

Any biscuit will do. Cover it with plenty of bath sealant You must use the smelly sort that dries quickly.

(Grown-up help needed here. They may not want to do it, but tell them they can trick THEIR friends as well and they'll jump to it fast enough.)

When the sealant has dried, remove the biscuit.

You now have a perfect mould of the biscuit.

Pour some plaster of Paris into the mould. When it has set, in 30 minutes, take it out and paint it. Choc-chip cookies are particularly smart because you can paint the choc chips brown – makes it look even more real.

Just leave the biscuit somewhere tempting. Sooner or later someone will try to eat it.

NEEDS:- BISCUITS, BATH SEALANT, PLASTER OF PARIS, PAINT

CEREAL KILLER

Life is too short to question
everything, especially at breakfast.
Make breakfast for your victim.
Make a big show of doing everything
– put the bowl of cereal on the table,
with the spoon already in it
(important, that). Pour on the milk,
sprinkle the sugar, then sit back and
bask in the warmth of the gratitude.
What a surprise, the spoon's not a
spoon at all ... it's a fork!

NEEDS:- BOWL OF CEREAL, MILK, SUGAR, FORK

PAPER PICKLE

Get to the newspaper before anyone else. Keep
the cover, but swap the inner pages for
yesterday's paper.

Dad will take it for granted it's today's paper.

The trick may never be spotted.

ULTIMATE DETERGENT

Why not squeeze washing-up liquid all over your nearest and dearest.

Find an old detergent bottle and remove the top. Wash it all out thoroughly in warm water so that there's no detergent left. Let it dry.

Find about 40 cm of string, just thin enough to fit the nozzle. Push it right through and knot both ends.

Shove the string into the bottle and replace the top.

Trot up to your victim, waving the bottle and say "Shall I clean that off for you?"

Before they can say "Clean what off?", squeeze the bottle all over them. What comes out looks like detergent.

Good clean fun!

MYSTERIOUS PAPER CUT

Cut a piece of plain paper exactly like this:

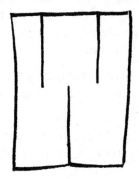

Now fold it like this:

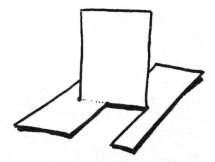

Just leave it around. Anyone who finds it will realize it's impossible!

FLOATING PEN

Although it's useful to have four fingers, we seem to have difficulty counting them. That's why cartoonists usually don't bother to draw more than three on a hand – nobody notices anything wrong. (Check the hands in this book.)

Here's more proof. Hold a stick in your hand. Grip your wrist with the other hand. Let go of the stick ... it floats!

What your victim doesn't see: your index finger sneaks up to hold the stick, leaving three fingers to grip the wrist. Nobody notices.

This works with spoons, sticks, rulers ... the bigger the better.

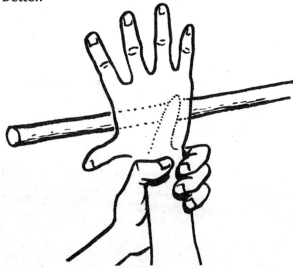

SECRECY

It is vital to keep security tight. Nobody must know your secrets, not what you've got planned, nor when you're going to do it, or who you're going to do it to. Here are a few hints to help keep security tight.

The most important secret of all is...

It's mo_____rtant
secrets_____one
can see_____tiality
is confi

NOW YOU SEE M, NOW YOU DON'T

A neat way to pass messages which you can read instantly, but nobody else can see.

What does this say?

To find out

- Don't look at the shapes
- Look at the spaces in between
- It helps if you draw a line across the top and bottom.

NVWLS

Surprisingly, it is possible to understand English even if half of it is missing. If you take away all the vowels, it is still possible to understand a sentence. For instance, what does this say?

FR NSTNCE, WHT DS THS SY?

If you take away the gaps in between the words it is STILL possible to make sense of it – try this:

TSSMPLJBTRDTHSSNTNC.

See p192 for answer

DOG LATIN

You and your friends can speak to each other but nobody else can understand you.

Simply stick "aig" in the middle of each syllable.

Syllables are the beats in each word. "Banana" has three syllables. Each syllable starts with a consonant, followed by a vowel. Put an "aig" after the consonant and before the vowel.

"Ba-na-na" becomes

"B**aig**a-n**aig**a-n**aig**a".

"Cat sat on the mat" is now

"C**aig**at s**aig**at **aig**on th**aig**e m**aig**at".

Yes, it takes time to understand it, but if two of you can speak it, you have your own secret language.

INVISIBLE INK

Using an old fountain pen or a paintbrush, write a message on paper in lemon juice. When it dries it's invisible – the paper looks blank.

When it's cooked under the grill or in the toaster for a few seconds, the lemon turns brown.

VOILA!

SIGN LANGUAGE

This is the language used by deaf people. Learn it and you can "talk" to each other even across a football stadium.

SECRET BOOK SAFE

Keep your most prized possessions out of the way.
Cut a hole out of the centre of a book and store
them there.

(You will probably need a grown-up to help you do
the cutting).

Warning! You need a thick book. And make sure
you've finished with it. Reading a book with no
middle can be frustrating.

BURGLAR ALARMS

Protect your secrets.

Sound Advice

Make a pile of noisy things, balanced one atop the other. Leave it right behind your door, so you can just squeeze out. Anyone sneaking into your room will knock it over, and the whole house will know about it.

THE LOONY BALLOONY

Not so noisy, but just as tasty. Blow up a balloon and squeeze it between the door and the frame. (If it's not a tight fit, wrap it round with some tissue paper to bulk it out.)

Next time someone goes into your room they'll get the shock of their life.

HAS ANYONE BEEN THERE?

Two sure-fire ways to check if anyone has been meddling in your room:

1) Use some soap to stick a hair across the gap of your cupboard door. Anyone opening the door will disturb the hair.

2) The lure – leave your secret diary out on the bed. Of course it's not really your secret diary (that's the book called "MATHS NOTES"), but with that "SECRET DIARY" title, who will be able to resist rifling through the pages? And since you know exactly and precisely where you placed it, they'll never be able to put it back in quite the same place.

I SPEAK YOUR FATE

Every time they open their mouth, make sure they put their foot in it.

THE SIAMESE NATIONAL ANTHEM

Tongue twisters often pop into the conversation . . .
"Peter Piper, tum-ti-tum . . . She sells tiddly-poo . . ."
Mention this one:

"The national anthem of Siam is a tongue twister;
'Oh Wah! Tana! Siam.' It sounds easy, but try
saying it over and over, very fast."

Before long they are repeating clearly for all to
hear, "Oh, what an ass I am!"

WHAT A CARD

Give your victim a card. On one side it says

HOW TO KEEP AN IDIOT AMUSED FOR HOURS - PTO

. . . on the other side it says

HOW TO KEEP AN IDIOT AMUSED FOR HOURS - PTO

WOULD YOU ADAM AND EVE IT?

Recite this poem:

ADAM AND EVE AND PINCH-ME

WENT DOWN TO THE RIVER TO BATHE.

ADAM AND EVE WERE DROWNED,

SO WHO DO YOU THINK WAS SAVED?

When they answer, "Pinch-Me", you pinch them, of course.

NOTE ON PINCHING

There are ways to pinch and ways not to pinch.

Don't pinch them:

On the head (a) – too hard.

On the tongue (b) – dangerous. Too many teeth around.

On the ankle (c) – too far to reach.

On the bum (d) – you could be arrested.

Pinch them gently on the back of the arm (e).

"Gently" because you want them to come back for more.

DOH!

Tell this one to a friend:

"Do Re and Mi are the village idiots. One day they are all sitting on the idiot wall. Do and Re fall off. Which village idiot is left?"

FISHY BUSINESS

A kid was sitting on a railway bridge with a fishing rod in his hand. A gent passed by and spotted him.

"What are you doing?"

"Fishing."

"How many have you caught?"

"You're the seventh!"

HOW GREEN YOU ARE

If a red house has red bricks and a blue house has blue bricks, what colour are the bricks in a greenhouse?

. . . Think about it . . .

NOW ICY IT,
NOW I DON'T

If frozen water is iced water, and frozen lemonade is iced lemonade, what is frozen ink?

YOU AND YOUR BIG MOUTH

Hold your mouth open, like this:

Now say,

"THE ELEPHANTS WALKED DOWN THE HILL TOGETHER, THEN PARTED."

A BAD SPELL

How do you pronounce this:

GHOTI

It's pronounced "Fish" of course.

How so? Well

GH, as in "enou**GH**"

O as in "w**O**men"

TI as in "na**TI**on".

What about this one:

GHOUGHGHEIGHGHOUGH

"Potato", naturally.

GH as in "hiccou**GH**"

O**UGH** as in "alth**OUGH**"

GH as in "ei**GH**th"

E**IGH** as in "**EIGH**t"

GH as in "ei**GH**th"

O**UGH** as in "alth**OUGH**".

A PARADOX

Here's one for the intellectuals.

Give them a piece of paper. One one side is written:

> THE STATEMENT ON THE
> OTHER SIDE IS FALSE.

On the other side is written:

> THE STATEMENT ON THE
> OTHER SIDE IS TRUE

Now, if "the statement on the other side IS false" then "the statement on the other side is true" isn't true, which means "the statement on the other side is false" is false, so that means . . . hang about . . . what the . . . where's the . . . Oh, never mind!

NEEDS:- PAPER, PEN

ASKING FOR IT

A young apprentice on a building site was told to go to stores and ask for a long stand. This he did.

"Can I have a long stand?" he asked.

"Certainly," said the stores manager, "just wait there."

The stores manager went away. Half and hour later he returned, carrying nothing. "There, have you been standing long enough?"

A WAY OUT IDEA

The great nineteenth-century American showman, P.T. Barnum toured the states with an exhibition of curiosities. Crowds would queue for hours to enter the extraordinary tent, full of "real" mermaids, bearded ladies, grossly fat men, etc.

The problem for Barnum was that they stayed too long in the tent. The people outside became impatient with waiting for their go. The canny showman put up a sign at the far end of the tent, "THIS WAY TO THE EGRESS". The crowds thought an egress was an exotic bird, and went through the door, only to find themselves outside. "Egress", you see, is another word for "exit".

CARD AND BOUNDER

Here are three neat, simple card tricks, selected
from the 34,565,777,898,904 available.

"THE NEXT CARD I TURN OVER WILL BE YOUR CARD"

Arrange 21 cards in 3 columns of 7.

Ask your victim to pick a card, and tell you which column it's in.

Collect the cards up by scooping each column, keeping the cards in order. Make sure the chosen column is in the middle of the pack.

Lay the cards out again, not column by column but ROW BY ROW.

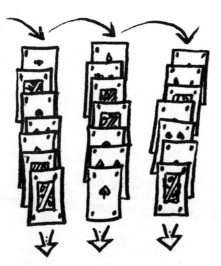

LAY THEM OUT ROW BY ROW

COLLECT THEM COLUMN BY COLUMN

Ask your victim which column their card is in now.

Again, scoop the cards up column by column, putting their column in the middle, then lay them out row by row.

Ask which column their card is in, then scoop up for the last time.

Your victim's card is now in the dead centre of the pack, number 11.

Now for the climax; tell your victim you are going to find their card from the pack purely by smell.

Hold the pack face down and lay the cards out face up, one at a time, sniffing each one; card number 1... number 2... ... ... number 9... number 10... number 11... keep going! ...Number 12... number 13...

"Now hold on," your victim is thinking, "he's gone right past it!"

Keep right on; ...number 14...number 15... Now stop. Your hand is hovering over the next card in your hand.

"I smell it! The next card I turn over will be your card."

"Don't talk nonsense," they say. "That's impossible!"

Reach forward to card number 11 on the table and turn it face DOWN.

MIND READING SUPREME

There are many tricks that use a stooge. This is the neatest.

Lay nine cards out as shown.

While your brilliant assistant, Claire Voyant, leaves the room, the others select a card.

Claire returns to find the card. All you do is point to the cards one at a time, asking, "Is this it?"

Claire says, "No...no... no... yes!" She always picks the right card.

How does she do that?

Well the clue is in the first card you point to. It acts as a map for the whole array.

So if you point to the bottom right corner of the first card, it refers Claire to the bottom right card of the whole array.

That's the chosen card. When you point to it she says, "Yes".

MEMORIZE ALL THE CARDS IN THE PACK

Riffle a pack of cards very fast. Look as if you're memorizing them at cosmic speed.

Now put the pack behind your back.

Each time you bring it out you show them a different card at the bottom, and you can tell what it is without looking.

Do it again and again... and again and again.

After you've told them ten or so cards they'll begin to marvel at your powers of memory.

But of course you're cheating.

When you riffled the cards at the start you memorized only one card – the top one. When you put them behind your back you simply shifted this top card to the bottom, face out.

When you held up the pack THEY could see this top card, but the next one down was facing YOU, so while telling them the name of the first, you were memorizing the second.

Back behind your back, you moved this second card in front of the first. Now, when you showed them the second, you memorized the third... and so on through the pack.

WHAT THEY SEE

WHAT YOU SEE

Bet you I can knock a glass of water on the ground and not spill a drop.

See p191 for the answer.

IT MUST BE MAGIC

It certainly looks like magic, but of course it's all down to your skill and cunning.

PAPER WALLET

Somebody asks you to borrow some money? Very silly! Don't just hand over a coin. Go further – make a paper wallet to keep it in.

As you fold each side round, and then the top, it seems that the coin is secure enough, but note that there's still a gap at the top. Hold the coin as you turn the whole kit over. Let the coin be felt.

Now, in the second before you finally hand over the envelope, loosen your grip on the coin, so that it drops into your hand. When the wallet is opened, the money's gone!

THE DOWN DETECTOR

Draw an arrow on a square piece of card, and another on the other side, at right angles to it.

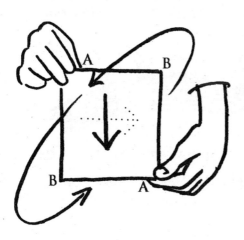

Practise in front of the mirror. Hold it by opposite corners (A–A). Show one side, then rotate it to show the other side. The arrow always points down.

Now hold it by the other corners (B–B). Now the arrows point both up and down. Hold it this way at the start of the trick.

To begin with, the arrow points wrong – sometimes up, sometimes down. But by flicking each finger, (and swapping hands to positions A–A at the same time), the arrow points downwards every time.

Suddenly your friend realizes that what they thought was simple nonsense is actually a bit weird. Give the card to them. Can they work it out?

TWO LITTLE DICKY-BIRDS

This is one for the kids – but lots of grown-ups are fooled by it as well.

Stick a piece of paper on each index finger. Show them over the back of a chair. These are Peter and Paul. You recite the poem.

TWO LITTLE DICKY-BIRDS SITTING ON A WALL.

ONE NAMED PETER, ONE NAMED PAUL.

FLY AWAY PETER! FLY AWAY PAUL!

COME BACK PETER! COME BACK PAUL!

On the "Fly away" line, each finger flies off and returns without the paper on it. On the "Come back" line they each fly off and return with the paper back on. How do they do that?

On the "Fly away" line you swap fingers. Look at the drawing carefully.

DODGY RUBBER BAND

Your victim will watch it for a second, think about it for a minute and struggle with it for an hour.

An elastic band jumps from two of your fingers to the other two.

What your victim sees: as you open your hand, the band jumps across from one side to the other.

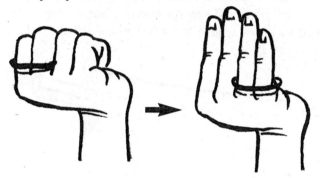

What YOU see (below): arrange your fingers inside the band like this and the trick is automatic. As you lift your fingers, the band snaps across.

HANKY PANKY

This works if you use a proper hanky, with a
seam along the edge.

The effect: a match is folded inside a hanky. The
match is then broken in several places, but when the
hanky is opened, there it is, unbroken!

Before the trick, push a match into the seam at one
corner of the hanky. Keep an eye on that corner –
you need to know where the match is, even though
you can't see it.

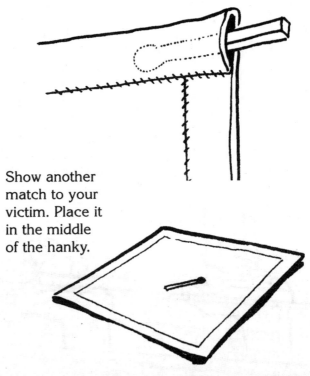

Show another
match to your
victim. Place it
in the middle
of the hanky.

Now fold over the four corners to cover it, beginning with the hidden match's corner.

As you fold over the other three corners, remember where both matches are located.

Pick up the hanky, holding on to the *prepared* match. Let your victim feel this match, then break it, then again – and again. That's definitely a well-broken match.

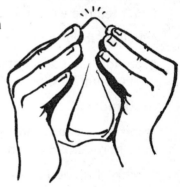

Now simply open the hanky out – there's the match, fully restored.

NEEDS:- HANKY, MATCH

WE'RE ALL IN THE SAME ZOO

This shows truly amazing magic powers. You need to do this to someone who knows their nine times table. If you do it with a crowd you can ask everyone to do their own while you concentrate on your main victim.

In fact, why not do it yourself now – this book will read your mind!

Just follow the instructions below.

"Please think of a number between one and ten. Don't tell me what it is...

"Multiply it by nine. Don't tell me what you've got...

"You now have a number with two digits. Add the two digits together. Don't tell me what it comes to...

"Subtract five...

"Find the corresponding letter of the alphabet – if your number is one, that's A, two is B, and so on...

"Think of a country beginning with that letter. Don't tell me what it is...

"Think of the second letter of that country. Don't tell me what it is...

"Think of an animal beginning with that letter. Don't tell me what it is...

"Think of the colour of that animal. Are you thinking of it?

"Now tell me how many grey elephants you think there are in Denmark!"

WOW! Not only your victim, but everyone in the room was thinking of grey elephants in Denmark.

How did that happen?

The key to the puzzle – if you multiply any number by nine, the digits add up to nine. From there on it's automatic. Subtracting five gives you four. The corresponding letter is D.

There is only one obvious country in the world beginning with D – Denmark.

There is only one obvious animal beginning with E – Elephant.

So obviously everyone will have the same answer.

"EXACTLY THE SAME"

Stunning powers of prediction, hem hem.

You tell the poor sucker what a brilliant mind you've got, so big that there's not enough room for it in your own skull, so you've borrowed space in everyone else's brain. Which means you can tell what's happening in everyone else's brain as well as your own, and here's the proof.

"Each of you has a piece of paper and a pen. I want you to write something on your piece of paper. Anything at all. I'm going to write exactly the same on my piece."

Impossible? Tell them to try. While they write, you write. Keep reminding them you are going to write EXACTLY THE SAME on your piece of paper.

When they've finished remind them again that whatever they've written, you've written EXACTLY THE SAME.

Ask them to show what they've written. Then reveal your piece of paper, on which is written:

```
exactly
the same
```

NEEDS:- PAPER, PENS

SHOW TIME

Let's give a big hand to these theatrical tricks. They may take a little longer to prepare, but they'll take forever to forget.

THE FAMOUS INDIAN SHIRT TRICK

An old Music Hall wizz-popper. It needs a little preparation, an old shirt and a stooge. (He needs to wear a jacket, so you may need to use a grown-up.)

Before the trick, rearrange his shirt like this:

When he puts his jacket and tie on, it will look as if he is wearing his shirt quite normally. Nobody will suspect a thing. He sits in the audience while you start your patter.

The ancient Hindu mathematicians of India discovered the secret of removing a shirt from under a jacket without removing the jacket! The secret was lost for centuries, but turned up last year in a car boot sale in Bognor. Here you see the ancient wisdom revealed once again in all its glory.

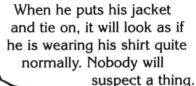

May I have a volunteer from the audience."

Your stooge jumps up and volunteers himself. Sit him down on a chair and stand behind him.

"The secret lies in speed and force, thus... Sir, would you please undo your cuffs..."

He does so.

"Remove your tie..."

He does so.

"Undo your top buttons..."

He undoes his buttons. Take a firm hold on his collar.

"Allez... OOP!!!"

Heave upwards. The shirt will come clean out of his jacket!

Now invite the others to try among themselves. If you're lucky, some of the poor suckers will give it a go. When the shirt doesn't seem to come, tell them to pull harder, give it more of a twist, etc. Many shirts have died in this way.

NEEDS:- OLD SHIRT, TIE, JACKET

LEVITATION BIG TIME

This works amazingly well so long as nothing gives the game away. Unfortunately there are many ways to give the game away, so practise carefully.

This is the effect; the high-flyer lies on his back on the ground and is covered with a cloth. The magician waves his arms and the flyer floats up into the air.

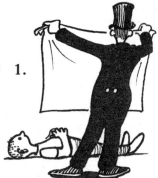

1.

BACK VIEW

And that's almost what happens.

1. The flyer lies on the ground.

He turns his head towards the audience, as far as possible. You'll see why in a minute.

2. The magician drapes a cloth over the flyer, leaving the head showing. Only the head. Not a millimetre of shoulder must show.

2.

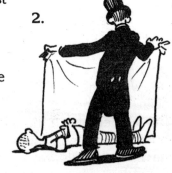

The magician can't just drape and go. The cloth must be held in front of the flyer, as shown, for a few seconds, because...

3. *Here's the trick. While the cloth is hiding him, the flyer turns over onto his front, in the press-up position.*

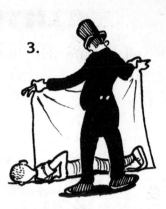

Make sure the head stays the same. Aha! That's why they had to turn it so far around. The audience can only see the head. If that doesn't turn, they assume the rest of the flyer is still on his back.

4. When the flyer is ready, the magician finishes the draping, waves his arms, and the flyer rises majestically into the air.

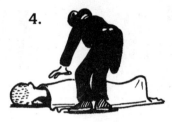

5. Actually he does a press-up, with one leg (the one on the audience side) held out flat.

The magician takes the cloth off in the same way – lifting it from the back, but keeping the front hidden while the flyer turns onto his back, (the head still fixed towards the audience).

The final flourish reveals the flyer as he was at the start, on his back, though a little air sick.

NEEDS:- CLOTH

A LITTLE LEVITY

Less effective, but a whole lot less bother
just to hover.

Stand sideways on with the front foot's heel hiding
the back foot's toes. Rise up briefly onto the toes
of your back foot, letting your front foot lift off the
ground. Wave your arms to make it look as if
you're floating in the air.

STRETCHERING THE IMAGINATION

A little bit of kit makes a wonderful effect.

Find two brooms. Hold them up with the business end away from you and the tops under your arms.

Get someone to put a couple of cushions or pillows on, then cover the whole kaboodle up with a sheet that reaches to the floor.

Tilt your head back and walk about like that. You look as if you're lying flat on your back, floating in the air on a stretcher.

THUMB PIN FUN

Stick a pin through your thumb and feel no pain.

Of course you must cover the thumb up with a hanky so the audience won't faint. And so they won't notice it's not your thumb, but a carrot.

Find a carrot the same size as your thumb and hide it in your hand.

As you drape the hanky over it – take your time – you hold the carrot where your thumb should be.

Now take a good long pin and stick it right through. Don't forget to moan in pain.

Take the pin out again, then remove the hanky (and carrot) with a flourish, revealing the undamaged thumb. A miracle!

NEEDS:- PIN, HANKY, CARROT

STAGE FIGHTS

Painless punches. You and a partner can fool people that you are having a serious fight.

1 – THE SMASHED JAW

The beast holds his victim's jaw nice and steady with his left hand while he pulls his right fist back.

He lets rip with a mighty right hook. Only he doesn't hit YOU, he hits his own left hand.

It sounds like a jaw-breaker. You jerk your head back and yell in pain.

2 - HEAD BANGING

He grabs you by the hair, flings you round the place, then crunches your face into the ground. Ouch!

Except it didn't hurt. He puts his fist on your head as if it had hold of a bunch of your hair, but it's completely empty.

You grab his wrist "to try to pull it off", but actually you hold his hand in place on your head.

Then you reel around, taking his hand with you. He does nothing but growl and look vicious.

Eventually you fling yourself to the floor, letting go of his hand. As you fall you thwack the floor with your hands, which sounds as if your face hit it. Come up holding your nose in pain.

3 – THE STOMACH PUNCH

He punches you in the stomach. You double up in pain, as you might expect. Except that he didn't actually make contact. His fist stops short of your stomach, but his other hand slaps his own chest to make the right sound. Your reaction "Oooof!" sells it to the onlookers.

4 – THE KICK

This needs practice. After you have doubled up from the stomach punch, he kicks you in the face. You fly back, spitting bits of teeth as you do so.

He, the kicker, needs to be very careful. You must be ready before he kicks.

What does "ready" mean?

Well, what he actually kicks is not your face but your arms. You should have put your hands out to "protect your face", but in fact you cross your arms in front so that his kick can't do any damage.

WARNING! Hold your fingers flat, to keep them unhurt.

He doesn't need to kick hard. Your reaction will make it seem brutal; you fling your arms back over your head and throw your body backwards.

Before you started this fight you put some mints in your mouth. Now you crunch them and spit the bits out into your hand as if they're your teeth.

CHIN UP

Look, I know this sounds absurd, but it really works. Really really.

Stick a dab of hair or fur fabric on your chin.

Paint a couple of eyes on your chin too.

Wrap a scarf or towel around your face from your nose up.

Lie upside down and trust me; your chin has just become a face. Speak, and your silly face speaks for you.

STOMPY STUMPY

Arrange yourself and a friend like this:

You wear a cardigan or fleece back-to-front. Your hands are wearing shoes, because they are Stumpy's legs.

Your friend sticks his arms down the sleeves.

Now work out a dance routine.

NEEDS:- CARDIGAN, SHOES, TABLE

TAKE A COLLECTION

Was it a good show? Take some money off the audience, whether they want it or not.

Take the collection in a metal tin, wastepaper basket or plastic bucket.

Hold the tin like this, with your fingers on the inside. Hide some coins under your fingers.

Show the audience the empty bucket. Now take imaginary coins from behind their ears. Pretend to drop the coins in the tin. Each time, let one slip from the store behind your hand. The audience hears the coin hit the bottom.

Rattle the tin every now and then. They can hear it filling up.

When you've emptied your handful. Tip the coins out and thank them.

NEEDS:- METAL TIN, COINS

CUT-PRICE COLLECTION

Not got a tin? Do it with a plastic bag.

Hold the bag like this, between the thumb and middle finger. When you flick your finger it sounds like a coin dropping into the bag. Now all you need is the acting.

Take imaginary coins from behind their ears, as before, but this time throw them into

the bag. (That way the noise sounds right.) They can throw imaginary coins from the back and you can still catch them. You can catch them a thousand fancy ways.

At the end, though, the bag is completely empty. You made the imaginary coins disappear. Big Magic!

NEEDS:- PLASTIC BAG

THE MARTIANS ARE COMING!

In 1938 in New York a young American director, Orson Welles, broadcast a dramatization of "The War of the Worlds" a science fiction story in which Earth is invaded by Martians. As trailers to the programme, the radio station transmitted spoof news reports earlier in the evening claiming that the invasion had already started. Of course they thought nobody could possibly believe that the Martians were really coming...

New York was reduced to chaos as the citizens fled for the hills.

The Chapter of Horrors

Those of a sensitive nature, stop here. These are the tricks that could get you arrested, or tortured, or murdered. Or worse; somebody might do one back on you.

PIE IN THE SKY

Tell your victim this is going to be fun. But don't say who it's going to be fun for.

Prop a bowl of water hard up against the ceiling with a broom handle. Now ask your victim to hold it there for you.

Then leave him! He can't escape without drenching himself.

Now comes the difficult bit. Let him off. Yes, rescue him. If you have any problems with this, read p6 – "Keeping Victims Alive."

WARNING! BIG WARNING! Make sure the bowl is plastic and there isn't much water; this could drop on your victim's head. You don't want to break either the head or the bowl.

HAND SHAKER

Here's how to lose another friend.

Ask him to sit with both hands face down on a table or the arms of a chair.

Now put a glass of water on each hand and ask him to get out of that!

Oh, what larks!

Careful not to do this in your own house – he might show you a very easy way out...

SNATCH AND GRAB

Give this book away – if anyone can catch it.

You can give away almost anything: this book, twenty-pound notes, CDs... How generous you are. All your victim has to do is catch it – and there's the catch, as it were.

You hold the book out, they open their hand, ready to grab. You let go, they grab... and miss! Because it always takes time to react to things – not long, but long enough. You can keep the book.

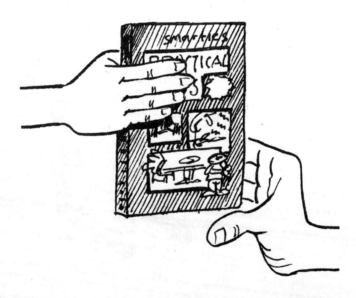

STRAW-DINARY

Give your friend a drink – go on, be nice,
they're going to suffer in a minute.

You both have a drink with a straw. Drink yours up.
Look across amazed. Your friend doesn't seem to
be very thirsty. Your friend is sucking away, but no
drink is going up the straw. "Oh well," you say as
you take away the drink, "if you don't want it I'll
have it."

How does it work? You pricked your friend's straw
with a pin before handing over the drink. Instead of
sucking up the drink, plain air is sucked up the
straw.

NEEDS:- DRINKS, STRAWS, PIN

BOTTLING OUT

Been cruel enough yet?
Take it one step further with this.

Give your friend a bottle. In it is something that looks like water. "What does this smell of?" you ask them. When they take the top off, water pours out of the bottom all over their legs. So that's one less friend to worry about.

What you did, you cruel, cruel monster, is prick the bottle at the bottom with about four holes.

While the top is on the bottle the water stays in, but as soon as they open the bottle the water pours out of the holes and soaks your ex-friend in the process.

PRICKLY TRICK

If you can't drown them, blow them up.

There are some brand new balloons in the shops. You can stick a pin in them anywhere and they don't burst. Show one of your remaining friends. Stick a pin in the top or in the middle of the bottom, where the rubber is still dark and unstretched. It won't burst.

"There," you say, "you have a go."

Guess what? When the unsuspecting try, it bursts. Har! Har! Another friend bites the dust.

NEEDS:- BALLOONS, PIN

GIVE AND TAKE

How to give a flower and still have it.

A cruel trick to do to a friend. So let's do it right away. Find a big, beautiful flower to give as a gift. Cut the top off just below the flower.

Hold it over the join as you offer it to your beloved.

She takes it by the stem. You take the flower.

LEVITATION

How to dump your friend – literally.

You need several co-conspirators. Tell your friend you are going to give her a ride right up to the ceiling.

Sit her down on a chair and blindfold her. Tell her to sit really still while she is lifted up. Your helpers grab a chair leg each and lift the chair about 5 cm off the floor.

Your friend has no way of knowing how far off the ground she's gone, so give her clues to convince her she's going up. Use a book to pass a shadow across her face, lower yourself as you speak, so she thinks she's rising above you. When she's touching the "ceiling", say "Whooooops!" and tip her off the chair. She'll think she's going to plummet to the ground. When she recovers from the shock be nice to her, or YOU will be in big trouble.

A-MAZE-ING

The human mind is brilliant at forming a mental map of the world around.

Lay out a simple obstacle course, give the victim half a minute to check it out, then blindfold them and set them to go round the course without touching anything. They will probably do very well.

But it's much more fun if, as soon as the blindfold is on, you and your friends remove all the obstacles. What a strange show your victim puts on.

Even better, they are sure of a high score!

NEEDS:- OBSTACLES, BLINDFOLD

STRATEGIC YAWNING

Set the whole train off.

Nobody knows why we yawn. The oddest thing is that it's contagious. If you find yourself on a crowded train, or sitting in a group around a table, start to yawn. Soon the others will begin yawning too. Weird!

STARES IN THEIR EYES

The simplest of practical jokes; the grandmother of them all. You can do this anywhere, and you need no props or preparation at all.

Just stare at something up in the air. Look very worried, as if it could be serious. It won't be long before you're surrounded by a crowd of people looking the same way. When the crowd is big enough, walk away and leave them to it.

WALL WALKER

A baby has walked up the window!

This is how she did it:

Make yourself a chocolate spread sandwich.

Press your closed fist into it. The chocolate sits on your fist in the shape of a baby's footprint. Now print it on the window.

Use your finger to add the toe prints.

Don't forget to wash it off after.

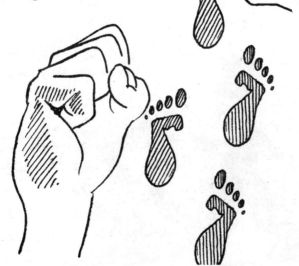

EARN MILLIONS OFF THE PARENTS

Surely it's not possible to get rich through pocket money? Oh yes it is!

Simply tell them you don't want any more pocket money after the end of this month.

But, just for this month, you want one penny on the first day, two pence on the second, four pence on the third, eight pence on the fourth, etc., in other words, twice as many pence each day. They will agree of course. The thought of never having to give you pocket money again will spur them on.

Whoops! Poor parents! In every sense.

By the end of the month you'll be over twenty million pounds better off. If you don't believe this, check it out on a calculator. Multiply 1 by 2, 31 times, adding all the results as you go.

THANKS, SON

GOTCHA!!!

Answers to the BETCHAs.

Bet you can't push me off a sheet of paper.

(See Betcha p86)

Put the piece of paper under a closed door. The big feller stands on the door opening side. You on the other. He can't reach you!

It's a pushover!

Bet you I can sing under water.

(See Betcha p64)

Hold a glass of water above your head and, to the tune of the Hallelujah Chorus, sing "Ha-a-ave I gotcha? Ha-a-ave I gotcha?"

Bet you I can knock a glass of water on the ground and not spill a drop.

(See Betcha p146)

Put a glass of water on the ground. Knock it.
Win the bet.

Bet you I can push myself under that door.

(See Betcha p54)

Write "MYSELF" on a piece of paper. Push it under the door.

nvwls answer (p117)

TSSMPLJBTRDTHSSNTNC.

IT'S A SIMPLE JOB TO READ THIS SENTENCE.